Persuasion

The Best Tactics to Persuade and Influence Anyone

Table of Contents

Introduction   5

Chapter 1: Types of Persuasion   7

Chapter 2: Solve a Problem   13

Chapter 3: Play into Beliefs   18

Chapter 4: Play into Fears   24

Chapter 5: What is the Straight-Line Sales System?   30

Chapter 6: Believe in Your Argument   37

Chapter 7: Develop Your Work Ethic   44

Chapter 8: Practice Your Pitch   50

Chapter 9: Make Opportunities for Yourself   60

Conclusion   64

© Copyright 2017 by Cameron Laws - All rights reserved.

The following eBook is reproduced below with the goal of providing information that is as accurate and reliable as possible. Regardless, purchasing this eBook is consent to the author of this book that any actions taken by the reader is in no way the responsibility of the writer and that any recommendations or suggestions that are made herein are solely for recommendation purposes only.

This declaration is deemed fair and valid by both the American Bar Association and the Committee of Publishers Association and is legally binding throughout the United States.

Furthermore, the transmission, duplication or reproduction of any of the following work including specific information will be considered an illegal act irrespective of if it is done electronically or in print. This extends to creating a secondary or tertiary copy of the work or a recorded copy and is only allowed with the express written consent of the Publisher. All additional right reserved.

The information in the following pages is broadly considered to be a truthful and accurate account of facts and as such, any intentional use or misuse of the information in question by the reader will render any resulting actions solely under their jurisdiction. There are no scenarios in which the publisher or the original author of this work can be in any fashion deemed liable for any hardship or damages that may befall the reader after undertaking information described herein.

Additionally, the information in the following pages is intended only for informational purposes and should thus be thought of as universal. As befitting its nature, it is presented without assurance regarding its prolonged validity or interim quality. Trademarks that are mentioned are done without written consent and can in no way be considered an endorsement from the trademark holder.

Introduction

Congratulations on buying your personal copy of *Persuasion: The best tactics to persuade and influence anyone*. Thank you for doing so.

The following chapters will discuss some of the many ways to influence people. Persuasion is a tactic that is vital to all sales but also plays a role in our social and personal lives as well. We must sell our products and more importantly, ourselves to potential clients and social ties.

You will discover how important the power of persuasion is to your success, whether you are in the field of sales or not. These valuable tools can be used to improve every aspect of your life in unexpected ways.

There are plenty of books on this subject on the market, thanks again for choosing this one! Every effort was made to ensure it is full of as much useful information as possible. Please enjoy!

Chapter 1: Types of Persuasion

Before we can delve into the concepts of perfect persuasion, we need to know what the purpose behind it is. For all intents and purposes, persuasion is a part of everyday life and will be used just about all the time. You may not realize just how often you go about trying to convince people, and yourself, of things.

In business, sales and marketing are the biggest fields requiring persuasion. The essence of both fields is to play up the strengths of a product to make it sound appetizing enough for consumers to buy. Whether you are selling a physical product, like a computer or TV, or a service, like an insurance policy, you must convince your customer that this product is the best out there and that they truly need it.

Everyone can be persuaded. There is not one person out there that can resist the power of persuasion all of the time. We are constantly bombarded with media advertising, and even when we don't realize it, our thoughts and actions are shaped by what we see around us. We hear messages from friends and family about certain products to buy and even how to live our lives. We are social creatures, and we tend to follow the general rules of society for guidance. For example, cell phones were non-existent back in the eighties, and we all survived just fine. However, one person persuaded another that this is the new thing, and now there is one in every hand in America.

When it comes to sales, there are tried and true ways to get people to buy, which we will discuss a bit more in the following chapters. By changing the ways in which you present a product and choosing your words carefully, just about anything can be sold. The key though is the way you present yourself. No matter how great a product is, a consumer will not buy if they feel uncomfortable with the person selling it.

Being a master of persuasion comes down to social abilities in most cases. We must be able to relate to our customers, as well as what you are selling. For example, say you are an insurance salesman, specializing in supplemental policies that cover what normal health insurance does not. Do you believe in your product? Is there really a need for such a policy when normal health insurance covers the bulk of what is needed? Do you have a policy yourself? You need to be able to show that your product is useful and that you personally believe in it (even when you don't).

If you generally get a little anxious talking to people, or simply don't have any sales experience, our first bit of advice is to get out and start talking to people. Making connections and utilizing social platforms drives sales. Most business travels by word of mouth, so utilize it. Even if you aren't talking to people about your product, you are still building rapport within the community by attending networking events and socializing.

Jumping into new social situations can be a daunting task for some. It may feel like you are totally out of your element even thinking about attending a networking event. If you think you are new to persuasion, you are not. Every day, we persuade ourselves to get up and go to work for reasons X, Y, and Z. We are able to carry out our lives because we have convinced ourselves that our plan of action will move us forward. Trying something new is nothing different.

Think back to when you were a kid, trying to persuade your parents that they had to buy you a certain toy for your birthday. This new thing was the best, and there is no feasible way you could live without it. You went on for weeks about this gadget, taking every opportunity to make your case. You were a born persuader, and somewhere along the line, you may have lost that confidence. Sure, your parents were probably annoyed with your constant sales pitch, but that is the tenacity you need to keep yourself relevant and present, so that sales may follow.

The rest of this book will be about more concrete ways to persuade people and improve your sales numbers. Really, if you want to have any success, these tips mean nothing unless you have the confidence and drive to use them. Get to know your product in and out. If you don't truly believe in what you are selling, make a choice now. Do you want to struggle to sell a mediocre product, or can you find something that you will have no problem personally backing? Often times, that is the only barrier to a great sales career.

Beyond sales, it is also possible to get people to like you through persuasion. The real question is, do you want to put up a façade for people to like, or would you rather just be yourself? When it comes to social situations, it can be very easy to put on a show, giving people the impression they hope to see. This doesn't always line up with the person that you actually are. It is important to strike a balance between overly friendly and your normal introvert self, at least until a person has a chance to get to know you.

Think about that one person you know that seems to get along with everyone. Look a little closer. They are probably pretty good at going with the flow and being generally agreeable. Perhaps they get along with people of conflicting morals and crowds. In the past, you may have envied this person for being so socially accepted, but think about what this says about their social skills. If this person gets along with all types of people, who have conflicting opinions and ideas, something is wrong. They have opinions of their own, which must conflict with someone. While people with different views can certainly get along, this person may not be confident enough to voice their true opinion, and would rather just be agreeable to avoid an argument. Is this person really strong? Someone, to be envied?

While it is definitely possible to persuade everyone to like you, what is the point? If you need to change your personality to do so, that hardly seems worthwhile. There may come times when the power of persuasion does come in handy in your personal life, but just be careful not to lose yourself in the process. Accept that some people simply will not like you, just as you inexplicably avoid certain people that just rub you the wrong way.

Chapter 2: Solve a Problem

Aristotle, the ancient Greek philosopher was made famous with his work in early physics and science but is also perhaps the first persuader in history to write a self-help book on persuasion. He explains that there are three main points to making a good argument, and perhaps the most important are the idea of "logos", or the power of your points of persuasion. That is, you must have great selling points to make the sale.

This idea transcends ancient Greece to the modern sales floor. The concept behind any good product is the idea that it solves a problem. For example, a mop is a clever invention because it solves the problem of a dirty floor. While that may seem simple, the pros of a product may not always be obvious, and it is your job to find those silver linings and present them to your clients. Why is this mop different from any other mop?

For example, if you were a car salesman, your job is to sell a specific make and model of car, of which there are hundreds of options. You cannot rely on the fact that said car will get you from point A to point B, as every reliable car will do that. Car manufacturers must constantly innovate new ideas to make travel safer, more comfortable, and more fun. The salesperson's job is to know what those innovations are and to find a way to let the customer know about them.

First, you must identify a problem. What is it that drives people to look for a product such as yours? As an example, let's use a service, like an interior designer. In order to develop an outstanding argument for choosing your firm, you must understand what people are looking for. Maybe you specialize in organization, eliminating the problem of clutter and chaos in all of the homes you touch.

Most people consider the field of interior design a luxury. You pick out color schemes and fabrics for the wealthy, who can afford perfectly-planned spaces. Framing your business in a way that provides a valuable organization service for the everyday person opens doors to future sales and lets your potential clients know that you are more than a color-wheel expert. How do you go about doing that in any field?

- Identify a problem
- Market yourself as a solution to that problem. If the client has termites, let them know you can handle termites.
- Set yourself apart. Why are you the best option for their needs versus the competition? What do you do differently, and why is that superior?
- Don't forget about the details.

This last one is vitally important. Most problems in life aren't so simple. If they were, people would be handling them on their own, rather than calling in a professional, such as yourself. Know the ins and outs of any problem that may arise to address the need better.

For example, look at the field of nutrition. There are many ways a nutritionist could help a client. One of the most common drivers for the client could be weight loss. If you look at the basics, weight loss comes down to eating fewer calories than you burn, so that the body burns fat for energy. If it were that simple, nobody would be overweight.

A good nutritionist knows the intricacies of a problem. This person could have a thyroid or other metabolic issues that make losing weight difficult. The client could have zero knowledge of proper nutrition and calorie content. They may have disordered eating patterns that make overeating a psychological problem. A true professional is able to address all of these problems that hinder weight loss, instead of just telling someone to stick to a certain calorie level.

Solving a problem is rarely a single-step process. For example, it is not enough to sell a person on the new features of a car. Having a backup camera and sunroof is great, but it is often financing that gets in the way. A good car salesman can walk their customer through the features of the car, as well as all of the necessary steps to get funded and out the door. They are not just selling a car, they are selling the car-buying experience. These days, many dealerships focus their marketing schemes on just that. Manufacturers put out commercials to sell their new models while individual dealerships promote their service, and why you should buy a said car from them instead of the guy down the street.

A great salesman will be able to find problems people did not know they had. This relates directly to products that are generally considered a luxury. If we go back in time a bit, most people would wash their clothes on a washboard out in the backyard. They would then dry the clothes on the line, at the mercy of the weather outside. Before electricity and modern technology, this is just the way things were done. People did not consider this a problem, just a task necessary for life.

The development of an electric washer and dryer was solving a problem people did not know they had. They didn't realize washing clothes did not have to be an all-day affair, it just was. Granted, the clever washer salesman had an easy pitch, but the point is, the salesperson needs to bring a problem to a potential client's attention, so they can realize that they do, in fact, have a problem.

Chapter 3: Play into Beliefs

Nothing cuts deeper into a person than their belief system. A person's moral compass is what guides them in their actions, and in turn, their purchases. In order to strengthen the argument for your product, you have to make a connection between a personal belief and what you are selling.

When we say belief, many people think of spiritual belief and religion, which can certainly apply, but in sales, it is more about moral right and wrong. For example, family is very important, and keeping them safe is typically of high priority. An alarm company has a great pitch when they play into this fact. They could present their case in an 'if, then' way:

- If you buy this product, your family will be safe.
- If you don't buy this product it concludes that your family is not of high priority.

Framing the sale in this second way is tricky. You would certainly not want to offend someone by outright saying that they do not care about their family. There may be other reasons why they do not want to buy your system. However, using a little guilt and implying that the customer might regret not buying the system for moral reasons is a roundabout way of saying the same thing.

You also need to understand a person's hierarchy of priority. While many would say that their families come first if your product does not fit into their top needs to accomplish that, you cannot expect them to buy right away. Know how important your product is to determine how quickly they should reasonably act to buy.

If you are struggling with finding a moral connection with your product, don't worry. The great news is, the connection doesn't have to be related to your product at all. You may recall a recent campaign in the motor vehicle industry. This company focused less on the features of their vehicles and more on the benefits of making the sale, by giving a percentage of the proceeds to charity. They are not alone. Many companies agree to give money to charity as a result of a sale. The idea is that the product itself may not be much different from that of a competitor, but buying it from the said company instead of someone else becomes the real draw.

Emotional connection is huge in sales, and playing into beliefs. We have all seen the ASPCA commercials about abused animals. They tug at your heartstrings and make you feel insanely guilty for not calling to help the poor things. That is carefully planned advertising. Yes, groups like the ASPCA do great work and make a lot of change in the world, and they know it. They play up the moral issues behind their work to make it relatable instead of trading a donation for a tee shirt. While they do this as well, it is overshadowed by the overall moral compass of the commercial.

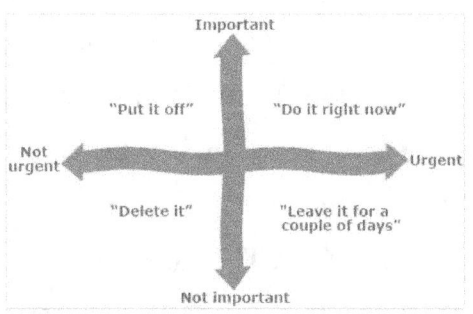

You may not have funds to make a commercial, and truly, it isn't necessary anyway. You can easily present your solution to a moral dilemma in person. For example, if you are selling an insurance policy, you could frame it in a way that shows why buying is good for the whole family. Here are a couple good examples that transcend beyond insurance sales:

- Buying this product will save your family from stress (with insurance, worrying about paying bills).
- This product saves time, which can be spent with the family instead (with insurance, fewer calls to fight over bills).
- This product will ensure the well-being of you and your family.

Getting the family involved is one of the most powerful persuading arguments. For all intents and purposes, no caring person would ignore the needs of their family by not buying your product. If it means more time with them and a better overall quality of life, that sale will be made. If you are not finding some sort of connection to the family with your product, look a little harder.

Of course, there will be products and potential customers that cannot be sold with the family connection. For example, buying a two-seater sports car hardly seems beneficial to a family with young kids. You could make the argument, however, that if mom and dad have this fun car, driving it will make them less stressed and everyone wins from that. Granted, you will need to play it a little smoother than that, but you get the idea.

Other products, like the realm of personal care, will require a different approach as well, but can usually be tied back to the quality of life. For example, our nutritionist friend could market her services as necessary for overall better health. With better health comes more energy to do more things you want to do. Maybe more things with the family? See how that looped back around?

Even things like waxing the hair off your legs could be seen as a positive improvement on life. Less shaving means more time for other things and more confidence in your looks. For many people, just feeling that they look good is a confidence booster, which can drive the success of their whole day.

Beliefs and ideals can be tricky, so it is important to know the limits of this type of argument. As we said before, selling a security system on the premise that not doing so means you don't care for your family is very dangerous territory. No matter the argument, think about how you phrase it before saying anything. Could what you say be deemed offensive? Are you overstepping your boundaries? If there is any question that you are, be careful and perhaps find something that is less controversial.

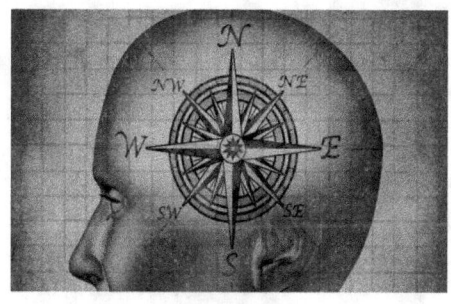

Finding the moral compass behind a product can be a challenge, but it is there. All products are created with the idea that it will improve upon something, otherwise, it would never have been made. It can solve a functional problem, bring pleasure and joy or make the user more comfortable in life. Present every product or service as if it were necessary for life.

This may take a bit of acting with consequential items like a kitchen gadget that is not necessary to live but would make cooking a little easier. If you present the benefits of say, an electric can opener, as life-changing and urgent, it will make the consumer feel that they need it. You know this works as evidenced by every infomercial ever made.

Chapter 4: Play into Fears

Along with playing into a person's belief system, using fear as a tactic for sales is very effective as well. If your moral beacon just started flashing, don't worry. We will not be asking you to be a fear monger, spreading irrational hysteria just to sell a product. There are definitely right and wrong ways to do this. Just use your best judgment.

Fears are often irrational responses to the 'what if' questions in life. We fear the unknown because we cannot wrap our heads around it. Common ones are, "What if I get in a car accident?" or "If I lose my job, how will I pay my bills?". The threat of something negative happening is a big driver for people. Without fear, everyone would be perfectly content and nothing would ever get done. In the context of sales, nothing would ever be purchased.

Fear forces the body into action. Physiologically speaking, our natural fight or flight response is meant to propel our bodies out of dangerous situations, like running from a wild animal. These days, there are more docile fears than physical harm, like how we will pay the bills without a job, or how to pay for college. For the most part, we have been reduced to financial worries, as modern technologies have largely solved our physical security problems.

Fearing that something bad will happen, or if you find yourself dead center in a crisis, stress hormones will propel your body into action. Financially speaking, the lack of zeros on your bank statement will prompt you to go out and find a job. If nothing else, you will tap into your resourcefulness to find a way to put food on the table and maintain a stable place to live. Everything else is really just secondary.

Having a product that helps solve a big what-if problem like this is a big winner. For example, services like accountants and financial planners market their services around planning for the financial future, helping resolve fears of losing an income. This service solves the problem of the unknown by giving clarity to the possible scenario of losing a job.

What about all of those little things that we cannot relate to a life or death situation, like buying the latest phone? Any phone will allow us to call potential employers or clients, so how can we sell the latest features based on fear?

The answer is, very tactfully. As we talked about before, we are very socially connected creatures, and we crave to be relevant in our social circles. While it may seem unnecessary, we like to have the latest and greatest thing to show our financial status and to make people envious of us. For example, if you wear old, dingy clothes out to a party, you automatically feel less confident as a person. If you wear a new dress or new suit, you gain all the confidence in the world. While this seems decadent and really shallow (which it is), it is a reality for many people. Creating the idea that your product is the next big thing which everyone will have shortly brings excitement and a sense of urgency to be the first person to have one.

We can see this phenomenon with new phones, and specifically, Apple products. We see on the news that people line up outside the store days in advance just to be the first in line for the newest gadget. The first in line is always interviewed, and they are always proud to be the first receiver of a product that is a dime a dozen.

This brings up another good point about fear in sales. Marketing something as a limited time offer, or implying that a product is in short supply creates the sense of urgency to buy. Make people afraid that if they don't act now, they could miss out altogether. Realistically, a company like Apple would not just make a thousand new watches. They would make them until blue in the face, and sell as many as possible. Supply and demand would be hard at work. Still, somehow the idea that you may not be able to get one is a scary thought, so why risk it? Buy now!

 Instilling a little bit of fear and urgency to push a product is commonplace. With that, we must be careful not to overstep the moral boundaries associated with that. Fear is a very powerful thing, and if brandished inappropriately, can cause panic and unnecessary problems. Fear should not be used to take advantage of someone in their time of need.

For example, think about the last time a major storm hit your area. It could have been the threat of a blizzard or hurricane, something that could cause a bit of destruction. Of course, the weathermen always play it up as the storm of the century, but their intentions are good, for the most part. They like to over-caution people to prepare in the event that something catastrophic does truly happen. Sales of milk, bread, and nonperishable goods inevitably rise prior to these events, but other companies feel the desire to take advantage by price gouging and hyping up the fear, even more, just to drive sales.

Use this general rule of thumb: If your gut feeling is that your sales tactics are unethical, they probably are. Think about how you would feel if you were taken advantage of at a time when you felt vulnerable and afraid. Would you be happy with someone who talked you into getting the biggest, most powerful generator money could buy if you could have lived with a smaller model for the basic necessities? Upselling products and price gouging during times of need is immoral, and will certainly come back to haunt you once things have died down.

A good, caring salesperson will always put the true needs of their customers above their own greed. Those who have this virtue during stressful times will be rewarded with future business and referrals because they are perceived as trustworthy and fair, not greedy and slimy. Do not be that person. You may make a few extra bucks to start, but you will lose out on the back end instead.

Chapter 5: What is the Straight-Line Sales System?

Unless you have been hiding under a rock, you have probably at least heard of the movie, *Wolf of Wall Street*. Leonardo DiCaprio plays Jordan Belfort, a real-life stock market mogul who made a vast fortune off of his skills of persuasion. He was a fast, smooth talker who could get anyone to buy anything. You may also know that he made the majority of his fortune through securities fraud and money laundering, which he did serve time for.

He is a prime example of the power of persuasion, but he chose to use his skills for his benefit only and disregarded the law. That being said, we can certainly learn from his tactics, but pick and choose out the positive influences while excluding the illegal parts. These days Belfort is out of prison and now runs a business teaching marketing and sales tactics through his so called Straight-Line System.

Although his career did not quite follow a straight line, his idea of sales tactics does. His idea is that any sale can be closed by a careful line of questioning. As with any sale, there is a back and forth between the salesperson and the potential client. He believes that the salesperson can guide the conversation exactly where it needs to go and get 'yes' answers to all of the little questions along the way.

While all of this is happening, you must also be following Belfort's three basic pillars of closing a sale. The first is to develop a rapport with your client. This has to happen almost instantaneously at the beginning of the conversation. Rapport can be a difficult thing to define and needs to be specific to the business.

In general, rapport is the ability for someone to trust you. It is usually built over time and can mean you have a personal, friendly relationship with someone. In business, it means that you are an expert in your field, and you can be trusted to do the service you set out to provide.

When you walk in to sit with a client, you must develop a professional rapport right off the bat. If this person has invited you into their space or has set up an appointment to meet with you, they have likely already heard something good about you, or are at least are willing to take a chance.

Don't demean this professional rapport by being late, or by wasting their time. This person is in your presence for a purpose, not to make small talk. Keep on task by getting started with the most important parts immediately. Don't shoot the breeze and discuss the weather or a picture on their desk. This is vital because the more you waste time, the less professional you end up looking. You want to get in and out long before this person has the time to reconsider their opinion of you.

Second, you are there to collect information. Every person can be a potential client, but not all of them. Ask specific questions that you need to know about the person to make the sale. Find out what the client's needs are so that you can then formulate your plan of action for further questioning after.

Determine if the product you are selling is actually something they need. Qualify this person so that you know early on whether this person is even a potential client. If they are not, that's fine. Politely end the encounter and stop wasting time with them.

Remember that you are out to build rapport within the community. Maybe you don't have the ability to help this specific person with your product. Instead of simply missing out on a sale, try referring them to someone that is capable of helping. For example, if you sell car insurance but the person really needs a different type of policy, refer them to someone else. Not only are you building professional courtesy within your network, that lost customer will remember you as someone who actually cared about their needs and can be a good source of referral income in the future.

When you do have a good fish on the hook, control the line of questioning. Anytime you are in front of a customer, everything you say should be leading up to the sale. To begin without being too pushy, tell the person a little bit about yourself to inform them about your business and to build rapport. Next, ask open-ended, yet specific questions related to your product to determine what exactly the client needs.

Once you have this information, begin selling your product. You want to do this quickly, but thoroughly at the same time. Give the person just enough information to follow the conversation, but without getting bogged down in the details. Most likely, this person is already relatively sold, you just need to push them off the edge they teeter on.

Keep the conversation focused on the task at hand. Keep your questions focused, so your client does not get off on a tangent. Try to phrase things so that the client can simply answer yes or no before moving on. For example, ask if they agree that your life insurance policy could ease their mind about their family's well-being and if they agree that said product is reasonably priced. Open ended questions can be great for finding out what the client needs, but once you have established that your product is right for them, it helps build your arsenal of sales ammo to use later.

The goal is to get the client to agree to all of the good points that you are making, so when you go to close the sale, they really can't say no. If they were so agreeable to all of the points prior, how could they possibly refuse to buy your product? Here is a quick rundown of the questions you might ask following the explanation of your product:

- This product will help you keep a cleaner home, right?
- And the price for this mop at $9.99 seems reasonable, right?
- Have you ever seen this mop in a store?
- Do you think this would make your chores a lot easier?

You must have a specific goal in mind as you begin the conversation. If you are in front of a client, you are there to make a sale. Everything you say should be guiding you toward a close. If the client says 'yes' to all of the questions, there really is nothing else in the way to change their mind. We have established that the product is great and that it would help them. We even set up some urgency suggesting that this cannot be found in the store. Since the price is right, why not grab your cash and buy one right now?

What follows will either be a quick sale, or a series of barriers to purchase. We will talk a little more about that in the following chapters. These easy sales methods have been practiced and utilized by leading sales teams across the country. They work.

No matter how you personally feel about Jordan Belfort, you can still probably get behind his methods to success. These techniques are simple and easy, and as long as you are selling an ethical product and really paying attention to the needs of your clients, you will have a long, successful career in sales.

Chapter 6: Believe in Your Argument

Whether selling a product or an idea, you must be fully invested, and believe what you are saying to make a convincing argument. What you're selling must be ethical and logical in your own mind for anyone to believe you. It's that simple. You must also have thought about every barrier to a 'yes' that could possibly exist to be ready to sell.

If you have developed your own product or started your own company, you probably did so because you had a passion for it. This makes life in sales a whole lot easier. If you are fully invested in the product you are selling, it will be very easy to determine its selling points. Most new inventions are things that solve the need of the creator. They had a problem, came up with a clever solution, and are now marketing it to others. They believe that everyone should have this product, without question, so going after sales is very easy.

Selling something that makes perfect sense to you is easy, but not always realistic. Some of us may be stuck selling something they don't have a passion for. In the realm of sales, people bounce back and forth selling different things. You may like the idea behind one product, then move on to something else later on down the line. Your passion for this new product may not be as fiery, but is it still possible to sell it?

Let's go back to our insurance salesman example. If you sell insurance but do not have a policy yourself, does this make you a hypocrite? Many would say yes, but honestly, it just might not be right for you. But you can still sell it, and that is because you can justify that it is right for someone else. Not every product is for everybody, and just because you cannot see yourself using it, doesn't mean that you can't have a passion for selling it to others.

For example, say you are in the market for medical equipment. You sell things from diabetic test strips to wheelchairs, and everything in-between. You are not diabetic and your body is mobile and able. This does not mean that you don't believe these products are going to help someone. The difference is, you cannot simply try and sell everything to everyone. You need to find your market and sell vigorously to the people who will benefit most from the product.

If you are reading this book, you may be struggling with sales, which implies that you may not be fully invested in the product you are selling. That's okay. You can still make a good living with what you are doing, you just need to dig in a little more and find your selling points.

- Forget about your needs and look through the eyes of potential clients. This is not about you, it's about them.
- What was the intended use of this product, and how could it change your client's life?
- What other benefits could it provide?
- Take the tag sale approach.

This last point is very interesting. Think about the premise behind a tag sale. One man's trash is another man's treasure. Just because you don't see the value in something doesn't mean the value isn't there. There are billions of people on this planet. What you are selling is bound to fit someone's needs, you just need to find those people. Not sure where to start?

- Relate your product to something that is going on in the news.

The best way to create a buzz about your product is to tie it to current events. This, of course, may not always be relevant, but take advantage of times when it does. For example, if you sell power generators and there is a hurricane headed up the coast, your product is vitally relevant, even if you don't feel the need to buy one yourself. Sure, you can live a few days without your electronics, but others rely on them for life. Oxygen machines run on electricity, so for some, having power is a matter of life or death. Again, you don't see the need personally, but someone else does.

On the flip side of the equation, you must also pay particular attention to the shortcomings of your product. This is just as important as the positive aspects. If you have your doubts personally, others will too. In this process, try to convince yourself, even with all of your own excuses, that this is a good product. At least, try to put a positive spin on it to help recover your sale. For example, you may know that a car you are selling has a tendency to burn through transmissions. However, you can highlight the fact that the manufacturer has an outstanding warranty that would ease the problem should it arise.

Say you are trying to sell a set of encyclopedias. Wow, do people even sell those anymore? Yes, there are currently college kids canvassing this area, selling books door to door. You have to feel bad for these kids. Someone out there has sold them on the idea that people love to buy books from strangers stopping at their homes. This person has likely learned a lot from Jordan Belfort.

Put yourself in this kid's shoes. They are fighting a losing battle with Google, and other search engines where people can instantly find the information they are looking for. The idea of looking in a book is dead. There really is no functional reason to have a bulky set of encyclopedias anymore. Or is there?

There are many arguments against the sale, including the size and bulk of the books, the cost, as Google is free, and the limited information of what is printed in the book. This really seems like a drag to sell. To knock on a door without recognizing these problems is like swimming with sharks. You will lose a limb.

Instead, keeping a good attitude about your tough selling situation is key. Acknowledging that there are holes in your story can help you make the sale. You know these books are becoming a thing of the past, and for some, that can be the allure. You never see encyclopedias anymore, and some people like collecting memorabilia. Some people have a hard time reading a computer screen, and like things in print. Many parents like to teach their children to look things up in a book like they did as kids, using the index and table of contents, along with critical thinking skills to find the information they need.

Those are all valid reasons to buy a set of encyclopedias. Yes, the market will still be small, but with a few of those positive spins ready to go, you can still sell them to the right people. Know your market, know when you are going to be denied, and push when you have someone on the cusp of saying yes. Then go home and Google to your heart's desire. It does not matter that you don't use them, just that someone does.

Taking some abuse and developing a thick skin for sales is an important lesson all in itself. Every great sales person hears 'no' more than they hear 'yes'. If you have seen Wolf of Wall

Street, you will not remember hearing too many 'no's' as the movie chronicled Belfort's rise to the top. But know that the reality is that for every 'yes', there are a hundred 'no's'. The only difference between a successful salesperson and a failed one is their desire to get that yes.

Chapter 7: Develop Your Work Ethic

The life of a salesperson can be very difficult and lonely. They generally get a bad rap for being pushy and overbearing in their pitch. The movie, Wolf of Wall Street showed how persuasion can make you wildly successful, but not the points leading up to that. Jordan Belfort's story is largely unrealistic for the majority of people. The reality is that you will have doors slammed in your face. People will be rude and nasty. They will definitely say no, over and over again. Being confident and keeping at it even when doors are slammed in your face makes the difference between successful people and quitters.

Instead of daydreaming about a single client that could 'change it all', focus on your daily tasks. First, being a salesperson requires a self-starting attitude. You need the ability to get up on time every morning and get started on your sales. Success does not come to those who wake up late, take their time getting ready and only get out there when the mood strikes.

You will never, ever be ready to hear someone reject you, so take that out of the equation. Treat your day like you were due into the office at a specific time, just like everyone else. Be up and ready when you say you will start your day, say eight in the morning. Eat, shower and dress to impress like you were headed to a board meeting.

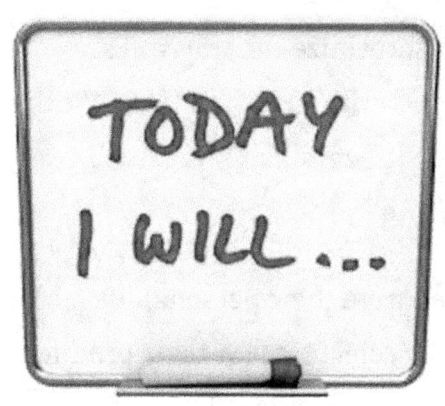

Establish a daily goal for yourself and write it down. Stick a note to your forehead if that is what it takes to stay on task. Make it something realistically accomplishable, like making ten cold calls, and following up on all of the warm leads you developed last week. To be quite honest, you can get those things wrapped up by 10 am if you don't dilly dally. Instead of feeling accomplished after that, push yourself. Set another goal, like doing twenty more calls before taking a break for lunch. Set the same goals after lunch. Put in a full work day. Cold calling in sales can be exhausting, so pretend that you are being paid by the hour to help get you to 5 pm.

Set some time aside each day to work on your sales pitch and strategy. You need to analyze whether or not your current tactics are working for you. For example, if you prefer to makes sales calls from the comfort of your home, but you are not getting the results you hoped for, change your plan. Try getting out more and see if that makes a difference. Also, taking just ten minutes to scrutinize the way you are presenting your product and critiquing it in front of others is invaluable to creating the perfect pitch.

A good salesperson can separate their personal life and work. That is, they do not take the rejections for their product as a personal attack on their character. You are just the person selling the product. If someone thinks what you are selling is junk, this doesn't mean that you are. Don't take it personally. Remember that no product is meant for everyone, so write it off as one of those occasions and move on. If you start to get down on yourself and lose your confidence, the rest of your day is shot, and the likelihood that you will quit altogether is pretty high. Just imagine that the very next person will say 'yes'.

In sales, you are the driver for your success, nobody else. If things aren't going as well as you planned, it is because of something you are doing. The good news is, it is also up to you to make the changes necessary to make it work. It is so easy to blame a bad product for your failure, but as we talked about before, if you put in some time to find the good points, it is possible to recover a sale. You may not be reaching your full potential selling a specific product. It is your right to continue pounding the pavement and making it work, or to make a change and move on.

Sales is very fluid, and very results driven. It takes a person with a very strong work ethic to stay with it. The positive though is that you can make your own schedule, manage yourself and reap the rewards for your hard work. You just need to be disciplined enough to take the tough steps towards making it work for you.

Many people say that good work ethic is just something you are born with. Some people like to work and others do not. The reality is, everyone's the same amount of lazy. The difference is, some people have the ability to force themselves past that lazy and get going. These are skills that can be learned over time, so if you haven't had the best track record in the past, there is still time to turn it around. Here are a few tips to get started:

- Plan to work every single day. You may not be working long, but even taking an hour on a Saturday to map out your plan for the week, or reading up on the latest in your field will help you propel forward.
- Just do the next thing. Thinking about your whole path of success all at once is terribly overwhelming. Choose what it is you want, and every day choose to do something that will further you to that goal. On bad days, it could be necessary to talk yourself into making that next call. All day long. As long as you do, progress is being made.

It helps if you love what you do, and that is hard to come by. Nobody loves their job all of the time, and that's fine, but you likely love something about it. Maybe it's the flexibility to work around your kid's schedule, to be home at a certain time, or to talk to people all day. Focus on those good things you look forward to instead of the daily grind and it will make starting the day much more satisfying.

Chapter 8: Practice Your Pitch

You need to analyze and prepare for every objection you can receive. The best way to do this is to practice on real people, who will throw you curveballs you had never expected. Having a well-thought-out answer to any objection will help you close the sale. Doing so has been proven to increase sales.

Trying to sell a product you don't know backward and forwards is a waste of time. Think about Belfort's principle of building rapport. You need to be seen as the expert in your field within just a few minutes of meeting a potential client. You do not have time to pussyfoot around your sale, you need to be on point right from the beginning.

You need to know everything, top to bottom so that when a client asks you a question, you do not even bat an eyelash. This may sound a bit overwhelming, but the ability to do this comes with time and practice. As you now have a strong work ethic after reading Chapter 7, you will know that you need to set time aside each day to educate yourself and work on your sales pitch.

This could even just be a few minutes to read up on the newest material regarding your product, or looking at reviews online for common questions and answers. While this is all great, it is also scripted. You need to practice in the flesh, with real customers. Only then do you have the pressure of the sale on you, which drives you to improve and think quickly on your feet.

Well, doesn't this sound like a confounding statement? You need to go into a sales situation knowledgeable and ready, but the only way to get that way is to practice by going into these situations. That hardly seems fair. Just like trying to get a job as an entry level professional, but the only job listings available are for applicants with years of experience, sales are unfair. That's just the way it is.

This is where your strong work ethic comes into play. It is not necessary to go into a sales job knowing everything. Nobody ever does. But you do need the tenacity and drive to get through that transition period in which you are learning. You will likely hear a few more rejections than normal, and that is to be expected. Any time you don't have an immediate answer for a client, you risk losing a sale.

You can make this process a little easier by keeping your cool. Instead of getting flustered and trying to answer vaguely and incompletely, just say that you don't know the answer, but that you will find out. Then do that. When you know the answer, you will have a second chance with that client, and you will learn a little bit in the process.

 Practicing your pitch is also something you can work on in your spare time. Some people find it helpful to actually write up a script of how their conversations might play out. Running through the script several times will help keep your talking points fresh and the information readily available. When doing this, pause to think about all of the possible objections and include potential answers to these problems in the script. If you are ready with an answer, you will be more confident, and the client will certainly notice.

Any time you get a customer question that is new to you, but a bit uncommon, write it down. Eventually, it will come up again, and next time you will be prepared with the information you need. For example, if you are selling generators, it is important to know how many appliances can be run on each size generator. Instead of overcompensating and trying to sell the biggest, most expensive one on the lot, be armed with the info necessary to help your customer make an informed decision. They will understand that you are trying to tailor the experience directly to them and respect your information.

Set a schedule for practicing, and make it something you do every single day. This may be taking an hour after lunch to do some research to find an answer, or simply creating an elevator pitch and running it over and over in your mind. You should be able to explain what you do to anyone within one or two sentences, known as an elevator pitch. It will only take about thirty seconds to get to your floor via elevator, if that, so be prepared to sell yourself in that time. You never know where you may meet a potential client.

Here's one as an example: Hello, my name is Jackie and I am a nutritionist that helps people find solutions to their weight problems with motivational interviewing.

This pitch tells the potential client who you are and your title. On top of that, it leaves a little to the imagination, prompting questions. What is motivational interviewing, and how could that work for me? The goal is to give enough information to explain how you could help them, but prompts the conversation to continue, if the potential client is interested.

This style of an elevator pitch is also great for cold-calling. You need to grab someone's attention in a matter of seconds before they even know what hit them. Just telling them you are from Generic Paper Supply Company is not intriguing, and you will be lumped together with the five hundred other paper salesman walking through that door.

Make your pitch catchy, interesting and memorable, but keep it simple enough so you say what you need to say quickly. Next, practice it until you are blue in the face. You need to have this memorized so if you were suddenly faced with an opportunity, you would not even flinch.

Now that your opener is down, you need to practice everything in between as well. Get the meat of your arguments down pat. Know your numbers and have visual aids like brochures and other paperwork available and ready to go if your client asks for something. Don't fiddle around in your briefcase looking for something. Know where everything is, be organized, and produce that media as if out of thin air.

More important than getting in the door is closing that door. Practice your closing statements over and over as well. Imagine that you have kept your client's interest all the way through to the end, and now is the do-or-die close. You need to be prepared to make a compelling final argument and be able to ask if this person is ready to sign on the dotted line.

You should also practice reading people to know if you have truly reached your close. It is easy to misread someone's agreeable attitude for an easy sell, then upon asking, find out, they were just humoring you to get you out of their office. There are obvious signs, like avoiding eye contact, shuffling papers around and fidgeting. It is okay to address this by saying something like, 'I sense you are uncomfortable accepting the last thing I just said. Would you like me to explain further?'. This way, you can address their concerns instead of just blowing past their uncertainty to land your closing argument.

Once you have your pitch down, backward and forwards, tear it down and start again. Analyze the things you are saying, the order in which you present your case and how you say it. There are always improvements that can be made, so don't just think you have it down.

Ask clients for feedback as well. This works well with clients you close with to find out what sold them, but can also work with a rejection as well. Politely ask if there was something specific that kept them from committing to the sale, so that you may strengthen your argument in the future. Avoid doing this if that client is rushing you out of their office. They are busy and trying to get rid of you. Don't make the situation worse by hanging around too long.

There is no such thing as a perfect pitch, so commit yourself to spending a little bit of time each day working on it. Try different variations, as people have different personalities and points that would grab their attention. Eventually, you will be so well versed that the sales will start flying in.

Finally, you must be able to learn when to *stop* pitching. Nothing is worse than a pushy salesperson. While you need to be confident with your pitch, understand that you will not always hear 'yes'. There will be definite no's out there and you just need to accept it and move on, instead of beating it to death.

Learn to sense when someone is fed up with your assertiveness and let it go. Every impression is important. This client may not have a need for your product, but could recommend you to someone else further down the line, but not if they have thrown you out of their office.

Use the same techniques you would socially in business. You know when a conversation is coming to a natural end, and the same happens in sales. If you have no idea what this is about, you may need to reflect on your social skills a little bit. We all know someone who just can't take a hint when a conversation is over. If you don't know a person like this, it is probably you.

Look for common social cues, like rushing the conversation, fidgeting and sighing to let you know when someone has lost interest. Save the interaction by politely thanking them for their time, and giving your card. Quickly, let them know you can be reached if they have further questions, or if they know of anyone else who would be interested in your product. You may have missed the mark today, but if you have not annoyed this person to death, a sale could come from the encounter further down the line.

Chapter 9: Make Opportunities for Yourself

Sure, you could follow the crowd and do what your sales managers have taught you. Or, you could be innovative, reinventing the wheel and opening doors for yourself. Don't be afraid to get the sale in unorthodox ways. Ask clients for referrals, and go out of your way to keep clients happy.

The mark of a successful sales person is their ability to color outside the lines. Everyone has a system, Jordan Belfort included, that is the 'perfect' sales solution. You could try all of the tried-and-true sales methods and never be successful. You need to find what works for you, and learn to work outside of the predetermined rules.

If you work for a sales company that has a set of guidelines and goals for you, that's great. They probably dropped a two-hundred-page script on your desk and told you that your success would come with memorizing the entire thing. Yes, using a script to learn the ins and outs of your product is absolutely helpful, but no script in the world is going to open every single door.

You need to learn to be flexible and seek out opportunities for yourself. While it is important to maintain certain goals, how you reach them is entirely up to you. This may mean that one day you are cold calling businesses to sell your new software system, and the next you could be hitting the links with a potential client. You are not tied down to a desk, and so you should have no problem getting up, getting out and doing what is necessary to drive the sale.

You also need to work your existing clients and contacts to drive your business forward. Nothing ever came to the person that didn't ask. People do not know what you do or know that you are looking for new clients unless you tell them that you are. People are generally oblivious and focused on their own needs, not yours. You may have a few referrals trickle in here and there, but real word of mouth business comes when you ask good clients and other contacts to refer you to others when they see an opportunity come up.

You can't always rely on people to do this for you, so sometimes you need to get bold and outright ask for what you want. For example, if a contractor would really like to get the job rebuilding on a lot downtown, they should not sit around and wait for their friend in the Parks and Rec department to tell the city building department about your exquisite work. Go down there and ask if your friend could introduce you to the person in charge of your desired project. You have already built a friendly rapport with this person, so it should be no big deal to get the introduction. Once you have that door open, the rest is up to you. The hardest part is getting the audience.

If your business is service related, like a lawyer or an accountant, get creative instead of waiting for customers to come to you. Professionals in positions such as this are usually pigeonholed in a serious role. Instead of selling the serious parts of your job, take the opportunity to get out of the office and meet with people in a more relaxed environment. Lots of people consider lawyers to be uptight, serious people and can be a little daunting to the average person.

Seize opportunities, like having a booth at a local Chamber of Commerce fair or farmers market to show people that you are human, and you are approachable. Instead of isolating yourself with people that already know what you do, have a more relaxed conversation about what you really do, and create more awareness for it. Get out of your comfort zone and try new things. The results will definitely surprise you.

Remember that sales is all about the tactics you use to drive clients toward a sale. Be creative, think outside the normal sales techniques, and get the job done. Don't be afraid to stick your neck out, but understand that a leap of faith does not always work out in your favor. Be gracious when you fail, and learn from your mistakes. If you don't you will be stuck in the same stagnant sales cycle for the rest of your sad career.

Conclusion

Thank for making it through to the end of *Persuasion: The best tactics to persuade and influence anyone.* Let's hope it was informative and able to provide you with all of the tools you need to become a powerful persuader. These ideas are great to promote a specific service or product, or to improve your personal life. We are all born persuaders, but somewhere along the way, we lose the confidence in ourselves to make a strong argument. Find that inner strength. Along with a solid sales background, you will be unstoppable.

The next step is to put these ideas into practice and start improving your life!

Finally, if you found this book useful in any way, a review on Amazon is always appreciated!

www.ingramcontent.com/pod-product-compliance
Lightning Source LLC
Chambersburg PA
CBHW050019230526
45470CB00003B/1046